Poems To Wear

From Japan and Australia

Poems To Wear: From Japan and Australia
ISBN 978 1 76041 206 7
Copyright Part I © text Noriko Tanaka & individual contributors 2016
Copyright Part I © translations Amelia Fielden and Saeko Ogi 2016
Copyright Part II © text individual contributors 2016
Cover design by Saeko Ogi & Mari Uchida
Craftwork: Mihoko Fukui

First published 2016 by
GINNINDERRA PRESS
PO Box 3461 Port Adelaide 5015 Australia
www.ginninderrapress.com.au

Poems To Wear

Contents

Part I: Poems To Wear	7
Lovely Kimono	9
1: The Age of Kimono	13
2: The Era of Western Clothing	36
Poets In the Order In Which They Appear	52
Part II: Australian Poems To Wear	55
Haiku and Tanka	57
Contributing Poets	105
Acknowledgements	107

Part I

Poems To Wear

by modern and contemporary Japanese poets

Selections and commentary by Noriko Tanaka

Translations by Amelia Fielden and Saeko Ogi

Lovely Kimono

Tanka and Haiku

Kimono tanka

> *whenever I wear*
> *a kimono patterned*
> *with spring blossoms,*
> *clad in their brightness*
> *I'm reminded of mother*
>
> Tanaka, Noriko

At the time of my marriage, various kinds of kimono were made to order to include in my dowry. These kimono were intended to last a lifetime, and to be appropriate for every phase of that lifetime. All of them, chosen with love by my mother, are of the finest silk. Even now, each time I wear kimono, I remember my mother.

My mother loved kimono, so from childhood onwards I too was often clad in kimono. Many Sundays we would go out together in matching kimono, mine a small 'waving-sleeve kimono' made from the same material as my mother's. Growing up, I too came to love kimono.

In the tradition of Japanese merchant families, I began learning Japanese dance from the third day of the third month in the year I turned three. But being too exuberant, I only lasted a bare half year before being expelled from the class by my instructor. Unchastened even after that, I started tea ceremony lessons and flower arranging lessons on the sixth day of the sixth month when I was six. Though I sometimes played truant, I did continue those lessons. From around the time I turned eighteen, I also studied koto playing, and I even became leader of my university's koto club… However, I believe all that was simply an excuse to wear kimono,

As I remember it, when I was a small child both my grandmothers wore kimono every day. To do the cleaning they would tie up their kimono sleeves and don aprons. My mother, who was still young at the time, usually wore Western-style clothes around the house; but unfailingly she wore Japanese traditional dress on weekends, and for excursions and special events. However, at some stage or other, even the grandmothers ceased wearing kimono. These days, it is safe to say, the only people who wear kimono on a daily basis are those who belong to a few special occupations. It is generally felt that the era of Western clothing has liberated Japanese women, mentally as well as physically. The other side of the coin is that many of our traditions have also been lost.

Kimono haiku

Mitsuhashi, Takajo (1899–1972)

> *wearing kimono*
> *do you wish for*
> *an autumn breeze*

Several layers of undergarments are worn beneath kimono; multiple cords tie the origami-like folds of the various pieces together; and finally an obi sash binds the kimono. Winter is no problem, but in summer wearing kimono is inescapably hot.

This haiku jokingly says 'you are beautifully dressed in kimono, but you must wish for a cool autumn breeze'.

1: The Age of Kimono

Types of Traditional Japanese Clothing

Awase

Awase is the name given to lined kimono. Awase are worn in the seasons when temperatures are low, from October to May. Not only is attention focused on the elegance of the outer material, but quite a lot of care is also taken with the lining. The colour of the lining reflects the wearer's age; and consideration is also usually given to its compatibility with the shades of the kimono itself.

Sugita, Hisajo (1890–1946)

> *with a spring-dyed collar*
> *it is fresh to wear,*
> *this kimono*

Awase kimono are worn throughout the month of May. With collar freshly dyed in a spring tone, it's like starting to wear a new kimono. Splendidly spruced up, the poet is evidently very satisfied with herself.

Hitoe

Hitoe is the name given to an unlined kimono. Hitoe are

worn in the seasons when temperatures are high, from June to September.

Hoshino, Tatsuko 1903–1984)

> *wearing an unlined kimono*
> *still a young wife*
> *she folds cranes*

Hitoe are thin kimono which give the impression of lightness. A young wife clad in an unlined kimono is folding paper into the shape of cranes. Maybe she's killing time. This haiku is somehow imbued with youthfulness.

Katabira

Katabira refers to a kind of hitoe (that is, an unlined kimono worn in summer).

Yosano, Akiko (1878–1942)

> *as cool as*
> *the skin on fruit*
> *is this summer's*
> *indigo-dyed*
> *katabira*

Katabira are mostly made of silk or hemp; the poet compares the feel of this thin cloth to 'the skin of fruit'.

Asa
Asa, meaning 'hemp', are summer kimono which in olden times were worn by commoners.

Yosano, Akiko (1878–1942)

> *how poignant*
> *the sound of cicadas*
> *when I start*
> *wearing a hemp kimono*
> *and at the height of summer, too*

When one can hear the crying of cicadas, there is a real sense that summer has begun in earnest. Hemp are everyday, informal kimono; they have better ventilation than cotton ones, and do not stick to the skin. Though they were originally clothing for the common folk, there now seems to be something coolly elegant about hemp kimono.

Ra
Ra, also called usumono, is a coarsely woven silk fabric, or silk gauze; for summer use.

Yosano, Akiko (1878–1942)

> *long long sleeves*
> *of silken gauze*
> *draping down –*
> *through them flit fireflies*
> *on the blue night breeze*

This tanka actually specifies the sleeves are two shaku, about sixty centimetres. A kimono with sleeves the length of two shaku conjures up the image of a young lady. Fireflies are flitting through the long sleeves of this thin maidenly kimono, and a pleasant evening breeze is blowing. Around her must be falling the blue-black curtain of night.

Suzuki, Masajo (1906–2003)

> *oh, silken gauze –*
> *loving the love*
> *that saddens*

Love can cause hurt and sorrow. Silk gauze kimono resemble greatly such fragile love.

Yukata

Yukata, summer wear, also nightgowns. Worn without an under kimono, directly against the skin.

Sugita, Hisajo (1890–1946)

> *the persistence*
> *of a stubborn woman –*
> *indigo yukata*

A poem about a Japanese woman who is a little obstinate and stubborn, yet charming. Such a woman is admirably suited with a clear-cut, indigo-dyed yukata.

Kawano, Yūko (1946–2010)

> *for Koh, now twenty-four,*
> *I bought a gift*
> *selecting*
> *a yukata with the pattern*
> *of blue morning-glories*

For yukata there are colours and patterns appropriate to the age of the wearer. Here it says that the poet chose a yukata with a design of blue morning-glories for her daughter (Nagata Koh), who had turned twenty-four. Morning-glories are classic for yukata, and give the garment the air of a composed adult woman.

> *I send Koh out*
> *dressed in the yukata*
> *of morning-glories*
> *whose story, like hers*
> *has a sad outcome*

This is a continuation of the yukata tanka above. Going out dressed in a yukata would mean, for a young woman, that it is some special occasion such as a summer festival, a fireworks show or a 'date'. Which would be exciting, not only for the young person herself, but also for the mother. So then, what can this 'whose story, like hers/has a sad outcome' be? For some reason, it is not a situation in which the poet can rejoice wholeheartedly for her daughter.

Kihachijō

Traditional to Hachijō Island, a woven silk fabric which is dyed with vegetable material. A special feature is the bright yellow colour of the vegetable dye.

Hashimoto, Takako (1899–1963)

> *the coolness*
> *of a kihachijō kimono*
> *chills me through and through*

When you put on a silk garment, there is an instant of chill. Kihachijō kimono also produce that kind of sensation. This haiku describes the feeling of coolness when one dons a kihachijō kimono, and says that both body and heart are momentarily chilled by it.

Natsubaori

A summer jacket worn over a kimono.

Sugita, Hisajo (1890–1946)

> *a summer jacket –*
> *so happy taking out*
> *my travel bag*

In recent times, one hardly ever sees a person wearing a summer haori jacket, but in Hisajo's times they were apparently worn frequently. Summer haori are made of translucent material, so the colours of the kimono underneath seem to float through, giving a very elegant impression. Their wearing season is from about the last weeks of April to the last weeks of October.

Summer in Japan is hot, and often women do not wear haori on top of their kimono. The main aim of wearing summer haori is to prevent the obi sash from getting soiled when one is out and about; plus they do smarten one's appearance.

The scene of this haiku is the poet preparing for a trip. There is an atmosphere of excitement as she gets out both a smart summer haori to wear for the trip, and her travel case.

Takeshita, Shizujo (1887–1951)

> *wearing a crestless summer jacket*
> *I am protected*
> *from the library*

'Crestless' means everyday clothing. Libraries can be dusty places, so the poet is probably wearing this plain haori to prevent herself getting dirty. A rather neat and precise style is also conveyed.

Haori
A jacket worn over a kimono.

Morishige, Kayoko (1936–)

> *my thirteenth birthday*
> *celebration haori*
> *with a plum blossom pattern*
> *I wore too this spring*
> *of my seventy-seventh year*

This tells us that the poet wore the plum blossom patterned haori she had made in celebration of her thirteenth birthday, and again in the spring when she was seventy-seven. In Japan, when one turns sixty there is a tradition of wearing a kind of red vest believed to signal 'rebirthing'; but this poet is going back to her girlhood at age seventy-seven!

Komon
Komon are kimono which have detailed all-over small patterns. They are worn as semi-formal attire, and for going out.

Nagamori, Mitsuyo (1922–2004)

> *my husband said*
> *the komon I bought*
> *is a dull colour –*
> *we spend the evening*
> *together in silence*

The komon kimono, which she had taken the trouble to buy, was criticized by her husband for being 'a dull colour'. The wife is shocked into silence, and the husband doesn't chat with her because he is uncomfortable.

Mofuku
These are mourning kimono in black with a single white crest on the back. In former times, the family crest differed for women and for men, with the women's crests being those of their birth families.

Ōnishi, Tamiko (1924–1994)

> *I returned home*
> *with my mourning clothes*
> *wet from the rain –*
> *the weight of silk*
> *soaked with water*

Maybe it had suddenly started raining. Silk always does have a kind of damp weight, but here it seems it has become even heavier with the moisture from the rain.

Obi

The obi serves as a belt or sash for kimono. Women's obi are very wide. A flat stiffener, called shin, is usually put between the kimono and the obi to make it sit firmly. Men's obi are much narrower.

Tanaka, Noriko (1967–)

> *I'm tying my obi,*
> *my queer black cat obi,*
> *for a tanka reading*
> *in the autumn*
> *of a foreign country*

Some time ago, I put an obi with a black cat design on top of the pale blue kimono I wore for the International Tanka Evening which took place at Manning Clark House in Canberra. That cat obi is one I had discovered and bought in Nara, when I was at the university there. Occasionally I wear this obi for going out to tanka gatherings. Then, finally, it travelled across the ocean with me to distant Australia.

> *a goldfish*
> *born from the flames*
> *swims*
> *the slender streams*
> *of my summer obi*

Dr Carol Hayes made for me a cute little goldfish of glass. Threading a cord through this, I turned it into an ornament for my obi. And then this 'goldfish born from the flames', flashing and sparkling began happily to swim the waters of my obi. At least that's what it appeared like to me.

Kimono Fabric

Momi
Momi is the name given to silk cloth dyed with red flowers. Formerly, red silk was often used for kimono linings. Glimpses of this deep red colour showed a sensual sheen.

Ubukata, Tatsue (1905–2000)

> *rip apart red silk*
> *when you are overcome*
> *with sheer jealousy*
> *which is strangely suffused then*
> *with the colour of red*

Momi is not an especially high-priced material. Moreover, it is easily torn. The scene of this tanka is of someone tearing red silk out of jealousy; together with the deep red image of the momi, it conveys the pathos of a woman blazing with emotion.

Parts of the Kimono

Sode/Sleeves

At the present time, the conventional length of kimono sleeves is about forty centimetres, but young girls' kimono have very long sleeves call furisode (waving sleeves).

Yamakawa, Tomiko (1879–1909)

> *will my sleeves too*
> *not return to the radiance of spring –*
> *a peony*
> *has been plucked, and*
> *laid beside a drum*

Very long sleeves on a kimono indicate a woman is unmarried. That the poet writes 'will my sleeves too / not return to the radiance of spring', shows her nostalgia for the springtime of her youth. The poet, who played the part of a younger sister to Yosano Akiko, was once involved in a love triangle with Akiko and her husband Tekkan, it is said. Eventually Tomiko was made by her parents to return to the countryside and marry. Later she met with an early death. Suddenly, within the breast of this poet who is threatened by a bitter fate, welled up a yearning to go back in time to when she spent her days with Akiko and Tekkan.

Tomiko is known to have learned drum playing in her youth. Thus there is a theory connecting the drum of this tanka to an actual musical instrument. I considered following that interpretation. However, in order to form mental associations, one must have the opportunity or experience of such things. And I wondered what it could mean: 'a peony…laid beside a drum'. Perhaps the tanka is talking about a flower arrangement? Perhaps it is referencing Kabuki or Noh drama? But I've never heard of such. The most likely possibility, in my opinion, is that the poet has written about the pattern on a kimono.

One often sees images of hand drums and peonies on classic Japanese kimono, the type of kimono worn only by young girls. It seems to me that Tomiko is gazing at a kimono patterned with drums and peonies, and sadly reflecting how she would love to return, once again, to the time when she was young enough to have worn that kimono herself.

Eri

As the eri, or neckband, is something which gets soiled easily, one puts a fresh piece of cloth on it each time one wears a kimono. It is customary to use white material for this, but sometimes it is fun to have figured cloth there instead.

Okamoto, Kanoko (1889–1939)

> *how coquettish*
> *is the neckband*
> *of my lined silk kimono,*
> *a little worn*
> *and softened with use*

Kimono collars get dirty easily. Here the poet says that while she was using a neckband made of winter-weight silk, it got soiled and softened a little. And yet she describes its rather worn out condition as 'coquettish'.

Kimono Accessories

Obiage

An obiage is a piece of material like a scarf, which is designed to hide the cord(s) in the gap between the obi and the kimono.

Sugita, Hisajo (1890–1946)

> *my new season's kimono*
> *with red obi scarf –*
> *kitchen work*

Kimono are season-appropriate, and the times for changing from one season's kimono to another are set down, too.

In this haiku, the poet who has just changed to her new season's kimono has attached to it a red obi-support scarf, and is standing in her kitchen. There is something cute and playful about this housewifely picture.

Obidome

Obidome, cord clasps, are ornaments attached to the cord which ties over the obi. Gold and silver, coral, jade, and pearls are often used in the design and ornamentation of obidome.

Sugita, Hisajo (1890–1946)

> *on my summer obi*
> *I fasten a jade clasp*
> *then leave the mirror*

Cool-looking jade is ideally suited to a summer obi. The poet was apparently in front of a mirror checking her appearance. She attached an ornamental clasp to her obi cord, then moved away from the mirror. The image of a cool woman floats through this haiku.

Himo
Himo, cords are used on kimono and kimono undergarments. They are made of silk or synthetic fibres, in all sorts of colours.

Sugita, Hisajo (1890–1946)

> *off with my flowery robe –*
> *tangled*
> *in all kinds of cords*

To dress in kimono you need lots of cords. The cords come in beautiful vivid colours. It is hard work getting into a kimono outfit, and not a simple matter to take it all off again, either. If you undress in a hurry, you end up with multiple brightly coloured cords trailing and clinging to your body. A funny sight.

TABI
Tabi are special divided-toe socks to wear with kimono.

Morishige, Kayoko (1836–)

> *those socks dried*
> *on a peach tree branch –*
> *in the evening*
> *I take them down*
> *from a purple and rose-coloured sky*

The kimono socks must have been washed clean and hung out on the branch of a peach tree to dry. The phrase 'purple and rose' refers to the colours in the sunset sky. The scene here is of the poet taking in her dried socks while gazing at the beautiful sunset colours.

Geta

Geta (sometimes translated as 'clogs') are the type of shoes/sandals worn with yukata and light kimono. Underneath they have two square wooden wedges; because there are two they make a click-clacking sound when you walk. Male students often used to wear geta.

Takahashi, Awajijo (1890–1955)

in the training hall
are female clogs –
first practice

This haiku says that 'somehow or other, a mannish woman has come to the kendō (Japanese sword-fighting) hall, and is apparently participating in the first practice of the New Year.'

Zōri

Zōri is the name of the footwear that goes with traditional kimono.

Miya, Hideko (1917–2015)

> *a display*
> *of pale scarlet zōri –*
> *already*
> *distanced from me,*
> *that pale scarlet*

Most likely there is a pair of pale scarlet-coloured zōri displayed in a shop window. This is footwear for a young woman. The 'me' of the poem once wore the same kind of light scarlet shoes, but now that time seems to her long passed.

Juban

Juban is the name of cotton underwear for kimono.

Kōno, Aiko (1922–1989)

> *when I get out of the bath*
> *and put on fresh underwear,*
> *the sensation*
> *of comfort I feel*
> *is so sadly short*

When the poet gets out of her bath and puts on newly washed fresh cotton underwear, she is momentarily startled into the realisation that in every generation women's bodies are always busy.

Tansu

Tansu – chests for storing kimono – are usually made of paulownia wood, because it is a good insect repellent. The handles on tansu chests, called kan, are often circles of elegantly wrought metals.

Kondō, Kasumi (1933–)

> *a late autumn afternoon*
> *when no-one at all has come,*
> *there's a sound*
> *of clinking handles – as if*
> *somebody is opening the tansu*

This tanka sees the poet at home one afternoon. Although no one else should be there, she has the feeling that someone has come and opened the drawer(s) of a tansu, making a clinking sound. It does not actually say so in the tanka, but that 'somebody' is most likely the poet's deceased mother; thus the poet's thoughts and memories of her deceased mother are obliquely revealed.

Kanzashi

Kanzashi are Japanese-style hair ornaments.

Mitsuhashi, Takajo (1899–1972)

> *a coral ornament*
> *in the matron's hair –*
> *sparrow wind*

A married woman is wearing a hairpin made of coral. 'Sparrow wind' is a seasonal appellation used in Japanese poetry to designate the south-east wind which blows in May.

Ōgi or Sensu

Ōgi is the old-fashioned name for a folding fan, also called sensu, which is used in everyday life to cool oneself, and in Japanese dancing, as well as on ceremonial occasions.

Nakamura, Teijo (1900–1988)

something suggestive
in the way
the fan is used

Folding fans are elegant. Certainly, playing with a fan in one's hand and hiding one's face is somehow secretive or suggestive.

Inaba, Akane

holding my tongue
I tuck my fan
into my obi

A sharp end to chatter. That certainly resembles the feeling of folding a fan and tucking it away into one's obi.

Kushi

Japanese-style combs, kushi are made of high-quality woods like boxwood. They are of finely carved wood, or lacquer, or mother-of-pearl; kushi may be coloured red or green, sometimes with coral or jade worked into them.

Ogi, Saeko (1931–)

> *picking up my comb*
> *from the path*
> *the gentleman*
> *says 'how beautiful',*
> *and hands it to me*

A man who picked up the comb for her said, 'It's lovely, isn't it?' and handed her the comb. A scene which makes one think of falling in love.

Make-up

Oshiroi

Oshiroi is painted onto the face and nape to make skin look white. There is both liquid and paste oshiroi. They say that, before electricity came into common usage, a thick layer of white powder gave the wearer a beautiful appearance in dark rooms. In contemporary Japan, this oshiroi is employed as make-up only by maiko, apprentice geisha, or dancing girls.

Yosano, Akiko (1878–1942)

> *Shijō bridge –*
> *a dancing girl*
> *with thick white make-up*
> *on her forehead*
> *evening hail lightly falling*

One Kyoto evening, a dancing girl wearing thick white make-up is crossing Shijō bridge; fine hail is striking her forehead.

Though the poet is the same sex as the dancing girl, she finds her an enchanting sight as the dancing girl goes along in the fine hail with her forehead held high. Reading this tanka reminds me of the Eirakuya in Gion. The maiko depicted on the Eirakuya's traditional hand towel is heavily made up with white face paint, oshiroi; she is wearing luxurious clothing and has an extravagant hairstyle. This dancing girl is depicted playing golf, rowing a boat, and skiing. She always looks tomboyish but somehow feminine.

Mayu, eyebrows

Sakai, Kazuyo (1935–)

> *how fond I am*
> *of the purple 'miyako wasure'*
> *blooming in early summer*
> *its colour reminds me of grandmother*
> *with her eyebrows shaved*

I understand that Japanese women in olden times shaved off their eyebrows completely when they reached a certain age. In Kabuki plays, too, old women have no eyebrows. There is a slight colouration where they have been shaved off, I have read. Initially I thought this would look very strange. However, later on, when I saw the female impersonator Bandō Tamasaburō without eyebrows, I found him quite beautiful. I'm not sure whether I thought this attractive because he was Tamasaburō, or whether the eyebrow-less look would suit everyone. Nowadays one never sees any Japanese women without eyebrows. For example, even if a woman has no natural eyebrows, she will outline eyebrows with make-up. Yet the grandmother of this tanka is quite old-fashioned and must have shaved off her eyebrows in accordance with traditional ways.

Hairstyles

Shimada

Shimada is the name given to a hairstyle for young women, which is also worn by geisha.

Yosano, Akiko (1878–1942)

> *those traces of oil*
> *were from a shimada hairstyle,*
> *I realise today*
> *with plum blossoms scattered*
> *over the wall*

This tanka says, in effect, 'On a certain person's hair there were traces of oil, and I wondered about this; but today, when I realise that was left over from the hair having been bound into a shimada style, it is spring with plum blossoms scattered over the wall.'

In other words, she did not know that the person whom she met was a geisha, and now, today, she suddenly realises this was so.

Marumage

Marumage is a hairstyle for married women.

Natsume, Sōseki (1867–1916)

> *her hair bound*
> *in marumage style –*
> *scarlet plum blossoms*

Around the time that plum trees are blooming bright scarlet, a woman who had just married began wearing the marumage hairstyle, it seems. This juxtaposition of plum blossoms and marumage is really effective.

Hairstyle at the time of confinement

Miya, Hideko (1917–2015)

> *tying up my hair*
> *with a white hemp cloth*
> *in readiness*
> *I shall quietly*
> *enter the birthing room*

In the olden days, at the time of giving birth one wore white garments and tied one's hair up with white hemp. This whiteness referenced purity, at the same time resembling the clothing of dead bodies.

Washed hair

Yosano, Akiko (1878–1942)

> *when I untie*
> *my metre-long hair*
> *it loosens in the water*
> *but does not release*
> *the secrets of my young heart*

Japanese women in olden times washed their long hair in a big tub of water.

The meaning of the tanka is this: 'Loosened in the water the poet's long, long, hair spreads softly, but the secrets of her young heart do not come to the surface.'

Once upon a time, in the Meiji era, this poem heralded a revolution in Japanese tanka.

Yasunaga, Fukiko (1920–2012)

> *when I wash my hair*
> *behind my eyes*
> *is an upside-down forest –*
> *chased into it*
> *I will dwell there*

This tanka tells us that when the poet washes her hair, unintentionally she ends up thinking about something. The unpleasant thing here is an 'upside-down forest'. We do not know in concrete terms what she is referring to – perhaps it is an illicit love affair. Amidst a confusion of feelings while she is washing her hair, she is, as least for the time being, 'chased into an upside-down forest to live there'.

2: The Era of Western Clothing

Clothes

One-piece Dress

Ozawa, Kazue (1942–)

> *through the mirror*
> *in quick succession*
> *breezes passing –*
> *my back fastener*
> *doesn't close properly*

Maybe the poet is changing her clothes in front of a mirror. The wind is teasing her, so she doesn't get the back of her dress done up right. In this tanka we have moved on from the era of kimono wearing; it clearly shows the current female dressing culture, which has become totally a culture of Western clothing.

Blouse

Muraki, Michihiko (1942–)

> *you stand before me,*
> *at the same time*
> *wearing*
> *a red blouse, and yet*
> *being a shy person*

There is a woman in a red blouse standing in front of the 'me' of this tanka. Although this bright red blouse resembles a large flower, the woman is really very shy. 'at the same time' is a logical expression, and 'and yet' is colloquial language. Actually this should give the tanka an inconsistent feel, but strangely enough it doesn't bother me. On the contrary, the language used accentuates the rhythm of the poem.

Kawano, Yūko (1946–2010)

> *my blouse*
> *illuminated by the sun*
> *of early summer,*
> *and within it the shimmer*
> *of my breasts*

The rays of an early summer sun are penetrating the poet's blouse, lighting it up. Inside the blouse, her breasts shimmer like a mirage, this says. The poet writes of her own young, sensual body, daringly likening it to something dazzling.

Skirt

Morioka, Sadaka (1946–2010)

> *what a dull world*
> *this is, complains*
> *my younger sister*
> *pretending to weep, while*
> *putting a skirt on her head*

This younger sister who is pretending to cry while hiding under a skirt, seems to be still quite young. Just reading the tanka we don't understand why she is pretending to weep, or what is so boring about her life. Perhaps, just maybe, the sister is saying that it's a bore to have been born a mere woman, always being told things like 'act like a lady', 'women mustn't do such things' and so on.

Chemise

Nakajō, Fumiko (1922–1954)

> *my chemise stolen*
> *at the public bath-house,*
> *I make my way home*
> *in the evening, just as*
> *the moon is peeping out*

This is about the poet going to a public bath and having her chemise stolen there. In Nakajō Fumiko's time, chemises were quite valuable, having to be either hand-made at home, or made to order. After the theft at the bath-house, she is making her lonely way home when the moon steals out.

Uniform

Iwao, Junko (1957–)

> *the student says*
> *he 'forgot'*
> *to put on his uniform –*
> *for them in general*
> *forgetting is OK*

The teacher asked the student who is not wearing uniform, 'What happened to your uniform?' And the student replied, 'Forgot to put my uniform on'. However, as an excuse that just won't do. We can hear the exasperation in the teacher's voice: 'Do you think saying "I forgot" about anything and everything makes it all all right? So is it fine with you guys, this forgetting things in general?'

SHIRT

Higashi, Naoko (1963–)

> *denied its desired*
> *evening shower,*
> *the sky*
> *embraces my shirt*
> *in a faint scent of watermelon*

'Sky denied an evening shower' refers to a sky dulled by clouds, and to humidly hot conditions. Under that cloudy sky, a shirt is drying. The tanka says that there is a slight smell of watermelon. One imagines the sweet, greenish scent a watermelon carries. It makes me reflect again how fresh are Higashi Naoko's tanka, far removed from the refined, high-falutin style of old.

Jewellery and Other Items

Rings

Sugita, Hisajo (1890–1946)

> *taking off my ring*
> *I suck out the bee sting*
> *with scarlet lips*

'Bee' is a spring kigo, a seasonal appellation used in Japanese poetry.

Here are described the scarlet lips of a woman wearing red lipstick, who takes off her ring and sucks out a bee sting. A haiku with an explicitly voluptuous feel.

Brooches

Kitazawa, Ikuko (1923–)

> *I think I'll turn*
> *my left cheek as well –*
> *bending my head*
> *I poke at my chest*
> *with the brooch pin*

This tanka indicates that a brooch is pinned to the poet's chest. There's a degree of pathos in the way the process of bending her head and stabbing at her chest with the brooch's fastener is phrased.

Perfume

Nagamori, Mitsuyo (1922–2004)

> *scents from the perfumery*
> *where I work as a guide,*
> *are on my clothes*
> *when I come home and*
> *wash autumn vegetables*

Apparently when this poet was studying in France, she did all kinds of part-time work. One of her jobs was as a tourist guide, and included taking groups of travellers into a perfume store,

French perfume has a fashionable, elegant, fragrance. Still wearing the scents of the perfumery on her person, the poet is washing autumn vegetables. At meal times the smell of a strong perfume could be off-putting, and even when one is cooking it would probably be a little too noticeable.

Suzuki, Kazuko (1936–)

> *to my earlobes*
> *which I've stealthily*
> *dabbed with perfume,*
> *the wind carries*
> *distant voices*

There are people who put perfume on their earlobes, and it appears that the poet is one of those in the habit of doing so. The tanka tells us that, riding on the wind, voices from far off were making themselves heard in the ears whose lobes the poet had secretly dabbed with perfume. This is a poem which starts from a narrow point, ears, and then gives the sensation of spreading far and wide.

Earrings

Nagamori, Mitsuyo (1922–2004)

> *my lobes sore*
> *from wearing earrings all day,*
> *I close the gallery*
> *and set off home*
> *through the night streets*

After wearing earrings all day long, her earlobes are painful, the poet says. This poet is the wife of a painter. Dressed smartly, she has been helping out at her husband's private exhibition. The scene in the tanka is this: night has fallen, she shuts the gallery and goes out into the evening streets.

Watches

Kubota, Shōichirō (1908–2001)

> *for my wife,*
> *to whom I never even*
> *gave a ring,*
> *I buy a Rolex*
> *at the Swiss store*

Apparently, when the poet was younger, he did not give his wife even a wedding ring. Now he is old and in easier circumstances, so as a souvenir of Switzerland he bought her a Rolex watch, the tanka says. Rolex is a top-quality brand favoured by Japanese people. Men of rank and fame often like to wear Rolex watches, but that deliberate purchase of a ladies' watch somehow creates an atmosphere of ruggedly honest masculinity.

Gloves

Shimizu, Mikiko (1926–)

> *last year's winter*
> *this year's winter*
> *the same*
> *purple gloves are*
> *warm on my fingers*

When winter comes, gloves are essential. The poet takes out the same pair of purple gloves she wore the previous year, and puts them on her hands. She seems vaguely surprised by their warmth.

Hats

Ozaki, Saeko (1927–)

> *one of the things*
> *I lost in the war*
> *was*
> *my straw hat*
> *with long ribbons on it*

Many things were lost in the war, and amongst them, the poet writes, was a straw hat with long ribbons. That wasn't 'just a hat'. It was a symbol of the poet's girlhood. What the poet lost in the war was not simply a hat with long ribbons, it was her rich and lively girlhood itself.

Kawano, Yūko (1946–2010)

> *wearing a summer hat*
> *a little on the slant,*
> *he looks down*
> *and then I see*
> *how long his eyebrows are*

A smart-looking fellow. He's wearing his summer hat a bit tilted. The brim of the hat covers his face, but when he looks down the poet sees his eyebrows, which seem longer than she thought they were. Her startled feeling is conveyed here.

Earrings for pierced ears

Miyata, Chōyō (1943–)

> *before dawn*
> *in a Shinjuku drugstore*
> *lining up*
> *is a woman*
> *with a ring through her lip*

When the poet went into a drugstore in Tokyo's entertainment district, Shinjuku, one morning before dawn, he apparently encountered a woman with a ring through her lip. Pierced lips are not all that unusual in themselves, but this tanka has a whiff of danger about it.

Scarves

Kojima, Yukari (1956–)

> *carrying the colour*
> *of that twilight long ago*
> *and far away,*
> *it no longer suits me*
> *my violet-hued scarf*

Looking at the purple colour of the sky at twilight, the poet is remembering something from long ago. Her violet-toned scarf which resembles the twilight does not suit her any longer. Generally speaking, one does not imagine violet being a colour to suit a girl or young woman. Rather, one thinks of it more as suiting a middle-aged woman. However, here it must be a violet colour suited to a girl. This tanka was composed with an acute sense of nostalgia for a time gone by.

Veils

Ōshima, Shiyō (1944–)

> *even now, it's fresh*
> *that sense of strangeness*
> *in the approach*
> *of a woman*
> *veiled in black*

This tanka recreates the poet's impressions of an incident when he chanced upon a gang of three thieves near a train terminal in Paris. The image of a black-veiled woman approaching in an atmosphere of strangeness is imbued with the aroma of exotic peril.

Sandals

Ōtaki, Kazuko (1958–)

> *standing here*
> *wearing sandals of blue*
> *I am as cool*
> *as if I gave birth*
> *to the Milky Way*

'As if I gave birth to the Milky Way' is a grand image of motherhood. The blue of the poet's sandals carries associations with the colours of roads and sky after rain, and of the universe and so on. The tanka is driven by a strong, broad-minded, rhythm. Sandals can be very smart summer fashion items, but the sandals of this poem, I feel, are the type of very ordinary sandals called tsukkake, slip-ons. There is a leap in images here, from ordinary, nothing special, footwear to the grandeur of birthing the Milky Way, which startles the reader.

Socks

Nagai, Yōko (1951–2000)

> *drying*
> *under a starry sky*
> *my socks*
> *resemble the wings*
> *of an exhausted spirit*

There is something forlorn about this tanka by a poet who died prematurely. We can imagine that the words 'the wings of an exhausted spirit' refer to Nagai Yōko's own inner exhaustion. At night drying under the stars, those two socks must have looked just like a pair of white wings.

Noguchi, Ayako (1987–)

> *no desire at all*
> *to be a teacher's wife –*
> *I wear*
> *navy-blue socks*
> *calf-length*

This tanka says that the poet does not hanker to become a teacher's wife. That's what it says, but I think it definitely means the opposite: this obstinate girl really did want to be a teacher's wife. Is the teacher she refers to a school teacher, or perhaps a tanka teacher? The wearing of navy-blue socks, calf-length, proves this is about a high school girl.

Manicures

Umenai, Mikako (1970–)

> *looking as if*
> *it will swallow up*
> *manicured nails,*
> *the peony is too large*
> *for a small garden*

A big peony bloomed in a garden. It is beautiful, but too large for a small garden, and it looks as if it is going to devour the poet's painted nails. In reality, peonies cannot swallow fingernails. Somehow the poet seems to be feeling inferior to the gorgeousness of the peony. Although perhaps it is that she actually feels inferior to some woman who resembles a peony.

Lipstick

Mikuni, Reiko (1924–1987)

> *the lipstick*
> *with strawberry scent*
> *is melting…*
> *I will become bright, I will*
> *become gentle, as you say*

Long ago, when I was a high school girl, perfumed lipstick was the fashion. Strawberry and peach and vanilla – all artificial scents with faint colouring. This is a kind of lipstick which symbolizes the lightness and brightness of girl students. Yet in this tanka, on the contrary, there is a somewhat cruel resonance.

The 'you' is telling the 'I' to 'become bright…become gentle'. The 'I' would like to be brighter, but she can't easily do it. Strawberry-scented lipstick is too bright; it's forlorn rather than bright.

Fasteners

Nakahata, Tomoe (1971–)

> *the fastener*
> *is going up*
> *my summer-lean back –*
> *this moon-coloured dress*
> *confines me*

Her zipper is going up, exposing a little of the poet's lean summer back. This is a scene which one often sees in film and stage dramas. It is somewhat startling. 'This moon-coloured dress confines me' has an em dash in front of it in the Japanese text. 'Moon-coloured' should really refer to something light and bright. However, for some reason, in this tanka one senses that it indicates the opposite, the darkness of night – due to the nature of the 'I' who feels confined by the moon-coloured dress. I find it a little mysterious, this poem: is the poet really shackled by the dress, or has she shut herself away in hiding?

Folding Umbrellas

Tawara, Machi (1962–)

> *as if folding up*
> *a folding umbrella,*
> *I change trains*
> *and arrive finally*
> *at my home town*

Folding umbrellas are unexpectedly troublesome to handle. First you have to close the umbrella, next carefully arrange its ribs and material, then roll it all up and finally put the umbrella back in its cover. In the same sort of complicated order, the poet changes trains several times to reach her home town, the tanka says. This metaphoric use of a folding umbrella is delightfully fresh.

Vinyl Umbrellas

Ōmori, Shizuka (1989–)

> *as if praying*
> *I open the vinyl umbrella*
> *at midday –*
> *I don't know even*
> *where you are*

This tanka is like a scene from a drama. Vinyl umbrellas are definitely not high class umbrellas, but this one is opened gently, 'as if praying'. At the same time the poet is thinking of the 'you', whose whereabouts are unknown right now...

I wonder whether this 'I' will actually discover the

whereabouts of the 'you'. No, it is more likely that neither the 'I', nor the 'you' exists in the real world. In this poem there is simply only an inspiration and a beautiful rhythm.

Tanaka, Noriko (1961–)

> *holding aloft*
> *an umbrella that looks like*
> *a transparent jellyfish,*
> *my friend arrived*
> *from Asuka village*

The transparent umbrella resembles a jellyfish. The way it floats softly through the rain is like a beautiful living creature. Holding open that umbrella, a friend from far-off Asuka village came to visit me. Why, at the time, I somehow had a feeling of strangeness was perhaps because of her being under this transparent vinyl 'jellyfish' umbrella.

Poets In the Order In Which They Appear

Tanaka, Noriko 田中教子 1967–
Sugita, Hisajo 杉田久女 1890–1946
Hoshino, Tatsuko 星野立子 1903–1984
Yosano, Akiko 与謝野晶子 1878 - 19042
Suzuki, Masajo 鈴木真砂女 1906–2003
Kawano, Yūko 河野裕子 1946–2010
Hashimoto, Takako 橋本多佳子 1899–1963
Takeshita, Shizujo 竹下しづ女 1887–1951
Morishige, Kayoko 森重香代子 1936–
Nagamori, Mitsuyo 長森光代 1922–2004
Ōnishi, Tamiko 大西民子 1924–1994
Ubukata, Tatsue 生方たつゑ 1905–2000
Yamakawa, Tomiko 山川登美子 1879–1909
Okamoto, Kanoko 岡本かの子 1889–1939
Takahashi, Awajijo 高橋淡路女 1890–1955
Miya, Hideko 宮英子 1917–2015
Kōno, Aiko 河野愛子 1922–1989
Kondō, Kasumi 近藤かすみ 1953–
Mitsuhashi, Takajo 三橋鷹女 1899–1972
Nakamura, Teijo 中村汀女 1900–1988
Inaba, Akane 稲葉茜 ?–
Ogi, Saeko 小城小枝子 1931–
Sakai, Kazuyo 酒井和代 1935–

Natsume, Sōseki 夏目漱石 1867–1916
Yasunaga, Fukiko 安永蕗子 1920-2012
Ozawa, Kazue 小澤一恵 1942–
Muraki, Michihiko 村木道彦 1942–
Morioka, Sadaka 森岡貞香 1916–2009
Nakajō, Fumiko 中城ふみ子 1922–1954
Iwao, Junko 岩尾淳子 1957–
Higashi, Naoko 東直子 1963–
Kitazawa, Ikuko 北沢郁子 1923–
Suzuki, Kazuko 鈴木和子 1936–
Kubota, Shōichirō 窪田章一郎 1908–2001
Shimizu, Mikiko 志水美紀子 1926–
Ozaki, Saeko 尾崎左永子 1927–
Miyata, Chōyō 宮田長洋 1943–
Kojima, Yukari 小島ゆかり 1956–
Ōshima, Shiyō 大島史洋 1944–
Ōtaki, Kazuko 大滝和子 1958–
Nagai, Yōko 永井陽子 1951–2000
Noguchi, Ayako 野口あや子 1987–
Umenai, Mikako 梅内美華子 1970–
Mikuni, Reiko 三国玲子 1924–1987
Nakahata, Tomoe 中畑智恵 1971–
Tawara, Machi 俵万智 1962—
Ōmori, Shizuka 大森静佳 1989–

Part II
Australian Poems To Wear

Girl in a Summer Dress

I cannot say it's just for me
this tender walking girl
now wears a floral summer dress,
but floating light and flowering trees
reflect the summer of her face.

A sudden season swings her heart,
the aching summer of her flesh;
where rippling flowers bend the breeze
and dance within their points of light
she is the suppleness of trees,
the open flower, bud and fruit.

And see this tender walking girl,
this shy and glancing summer girl:
her body's tall and slender tree
flowers now in a light dress
around the season at her heart,
its fragility and nakedness.

> Vivian Smith, b. Hobart 1933,
> from his first collection,
> *The Other Meaning*
> (Sydney: Lyre Bird Writers, 1956)

Haiku and Tanka

by 65 Australian poets

Selected and edited by Amelia Fielden

whose idea was it
that we should wear clothes?
imagine
how easy to care for
fig leaves would be

Catherine Smith

~ ~ ~ ~

neatly folded
clothes awaiting placement
in perfumed drawers
show no signs of seduction
by the wild wind

Jo Tregellis

~ ~ ~ ~

an arrest —
men with guns and tanks
fear
a woman of bamboo grace
with roses in her hair

Anne Benjamin

~ ~ ~ ~

have you noticed
on the after peak hour bus
the red coats
of the women going out
wearing their white hair

Lynette Arden

~ ~ ~ ~

hearing aids
helping her collect
their laughter…
what will help them
contain her wisdom

Carole Harrison

~ ~ ~ ~

teardrop
diamond earrings
the last waltz

Simon Hanson

~ ~ ~ ~

'four eyes'
taunts punches wire frames twisted
glass crunched
under bullies' feet
who can fix this for him?

Sandra Renew

~ ~ ~ ~

panda eyes
betray my misery –
a mistake
to wear mascara
for a funeral

      Jan Foster

~ ~ ~ ~

mirrored sunglasses
an azure sky
a turquoise sea

      Simon Hanson

~ ~ ~ ~

on tiptoes
the long bare legs
in a miniskirt –
'nice sunglasses'
says my father

      Belinda Broughton

~ ~ ~ ~

looking for mushrooms
I catch a spider abseiling
from my black hat's brim

Jeffrey Harpeng

~ ~ ~ ~

Sunday school girl
asks who made the world
who made
the bees and blossom
on my fruit and flower hat

Kate King

~ ~ ~ ~

foreclosure –
hidden by the brim of his hat
the farmer's eyes

Mark Miller

~ ~ ~ ~

into the garbage
my moth-eaten beret
from Sunday school days
yesterday's sins
come rushing back

Barbara A. Taylor

~ ~ ~ ~

conical hat –
one handful of seedlings
after another

Greg Piko

~ ~ ~ ~

four-inch spiky heels
sinking into the grass
she's two bottles down –
her fascinator breaking
snaps like a horse's leg

Penelope Cottier

~ ~ ~ ~

I watch her
peer between layers
of black veil…
eyes flaring
pale as marsh fire

Marilyn Humbert

~ ~ ~ ~

between black-stockinged knees
and strapless patent leather shoes
a hand strokes the cello
as the bridegroom's fingers
lift his betrothed's white veil

David Gilbey

~ ~ ~ ~

birds in flight
tattooed on her shoulder
winging it

Gail Hennessy

~ ~ ~ ~

a floral scarf
unfurls beside the road
as we travel
wild flowers are blooming,
paddocks dressed for spring

Jan Foster

~ ~ ~ ~

street style
individual egos
break away

                    Teresa Ingram

~ ~ ~ ~

a pit bull terrier
and the girl with spiked hair
saunter
down struggle street
in matching stud collars

                    Marilyn Humbert

~ ~ ~ ~

aunt's lace collars
so very out of fashion
but she persists…
the strength of self
in a world of choices

Dawn Bruce

~ ~ ~ ~

one small lead
and three large collars
in my cupboard
all that's left of thirty years
of unconditional love

Joanne Watcyn-Jones

~ ~ ~ ~

this baby
fingering the locket
at my neck
breaks into
inexplicable tears

Belinda Broughton

~ ~ ~ ~

on the hills hoist
a necklace
of raindrops

Margaret Mahony

~ ~ ~ ~

my mother-in-law's
red toothed coral necklace
tight around my throat
unforgiving of the past…
the reef whispers 'want it back'

Janette Pieloor

~ ~ ~ ~

crumbling
into the love story
buttonhole rose

Marietta McGregor

~ ~ ~ ~

dressed in her best
with hat and gloves of course
for the city visit
stockings fastened, well shod
the 50s lady steps out

Lois Holland

~ ~ ~ ~

rush hour…
a dribble of porridge
down a lapel

Scott Thouard

~ ~ ~ ~

it pays to study
the form on Melbourne Cup day –
winning jockey
the first time a woman, wore
suffragettes' mauve white and green

Jan Dean

autumn carnival
you strut through the bookies' ring
in your shot silk tie –
it seems that once again
I've bet on the wrong horse

Beverley George

on their break
in black franchise shirts
back to back
at adjacent tables
a dad and his teenaged son

Rodney Williams

~ ~ ~ ~

purple-patterned
the worn shirt lurks
in my wardrobe
dad's gift to me
many years ago

Maria Encarnacao

~ ~ ~ ~

balloons in the wind
a clothesline of white shirts
for his next flight

Beatrice Yell

~ ~ ~ ~

a Hawaiian shirt
calls out with shock value
in a city crowd
so many of us happy
to see it on someone else

Margaret Owen Ruckert

~ ~ ~ ~

punching an Other hOle in this Old belt

Jeffrey Harpeng

~ ~ ~ ~

belts with buckles
across the dressing table
beads and bling –
her latest accessory
the blood pressure monitor

Rodney Williams

~ ~ ~ ~

twilight
his breath warm
as he fastens my zip

Vanessa Proctor

~ ~ ~ ~

full skirt
favourite flatties
bobby socks
the going gear back then –
and we knew it all

Lois Holland

~~~~

my dress has faded
does it matter where I sit
to ponder the lilies

Jane Le Rossignol

~~~~

she slips
into something more
comfortable –
out of her tight skirt
into her garden

Barbara Curnow

~~~~

my mother told me
dad said she'd even look good
in a chaff bag –
from a mounted policeman
the finest compliment

      Jan Dean

----

embraced by the wind
her modest long flowing dress
reveals all her curves

      Rupert Summerson

----

never one for black
she selects a frock
for his funeral
the red of passion
the gold of sunsets

      Carmel Summers

----

grandmother
wore black lace-up boots
lisle stockings
and an ankle-length dress
onto the Bondi sands

Margaret Owen Ruckert

~ ~ ~ ~

our father
never to be forgotten
in mother's blue dress
calls out his own name
in her endearing tones

Athena Zaknic

~ ~ ~ ~

modern exec:
tailored black suit
designer shirt
club tie neatly knotted…
on his feet shiny red shoes

Cynthia Rowe

retirement –
an op shop dummy
wears my suit

Beverley George

home
from my retirement party
a little sad
for the very first time
at taking off my tie

Michael Thorley

eastern spinebill
in smart tan suit and collar
ready for the day
he waits in an almond tree
to work in the grevilleas

Paul Williamson

large footprints…
like a proud hotel man
in blue vest
and black tuxedo
the swamp hen walks away

Saeko Ogi

dressed in fairy wings
tea cosy and flippers,
self-consciousness
an unformed cloud
in a faraway sky

Catherine McGrath

~ ~ ~ ~

new party dress
four-year-old fizzes
into fairyland

Glenys Ferguson

~ ~ ~ ~

no wonder
the world is full of conflict…
dancing in playpens
plastic-gun-slinging toddlers
in camouflage pants

Barbara A. Taylor

~ ~ ~ ~

shop windows
full of gold-threaded saris
out in the sunshine
a pair of emerald dragonflies
wings spun gold

Jill Gower

~ ~ ~ ~

my first sari
of handwoven cotton
vibrantly purple –
now a zany bedspread
to dream in, cocooned

Samantha Sirimanne Hyde

~ ~ ~ ~

soft wool
hugs her tiny body
pink and perfect…
grandma's love
in every stitch

Crys Smith

~ ~ ~ ~

across the dusk
pastel pink knits a row
within the mauve
a garment for the hills
to end a mild day

Paul Williamson

~ ~ ~ ~

with care
she crafted each garment
stitch by stitch
threads not strong enough
to hold a daughter's love

Janne Graham

~ ~ ~ ~

sixteen
in the azure gown I made you
for your first formal –
only an emailed jpeg
to see how happy you looked

Anne Benjamin

~ ~ ~ ~

an old lady kneels
to adjust the yukata*
of this old lady…
softly falling
cherry blossom petals

Dawn Bruce

~ ~ ~ ~

a mauve mist
on a boatless ocean…
I fold all hope
into the chrysanthemums
of my new kimono

Hazel Hall

~ ~ ~ ~

* A yukata is a cotton kimono.

think of me
when you wear this haori*
he whispered
draping the silk around me –
I do, oh I do

Amelia Fielden

~ ~ ~ ~

our maple
wears its autumn leaves
lightly
I drape a cardigan
over my bare shoulders

Janne Graham

~ ~ ~ ~

* A haori a traditional Japanese jacket worn over a kimono.

in the op shop
moss-green corduroy jacket
I lust for
the precise cut of its lapels…
should fit my granddaughter

Gail Hennessy

~ ~ ~

ready at last
she hops into the car
in her rabbit fur
now orders carrot soup
and wild roquette salad

M.L. Grace

~ ~ ~

shedding grudges
with my overcoat
this spring
I prefer the feel
of your skin next to mine

Michelle Brock

I spin soft white fleece
woven from grass, wind and rain,
it kept a sheep warm –
next year I'll wear her old coat
while she will make a new one

Jane Le Rossignol

as I climb
Earth widens beneath me
the southerly
wind grows colder
shall I dare to wear a fleece

Gerry Jacobson

drizzled sky –
his blue anorak
brighter still

Mark Miller

she wore her sadness
like a melancholic cloak
as she told her story
I listened with great sorrow
shrouded in empathy shared

James Holcombe

old clothes sent abroad
shredded, woven, tailored
into combat coats
cover a new clash
on the north-west border

Christopher Dorman

~ ~ ~ ~

Paris survivors
in gold thermal wraps
stream into night light –
dazed, we search for shadows
in our own sunlight

Carmel Summers

~ ~ ~ ~

the three-gold bangle
came with a proposal –
I accepted both

Heather Gordon

~ ~ ~ ~

coloured beads
for every occasion
threading
thoughts to wire –
smiles for sale

Crys Smith

~ ~ ~ ~

removing the rings
from my dead mother's hands
the nurse speaks gently

Lyn Reeves

~ ~ ~ ~

in plastic bags
all his worldly goods,
the old beggar
watches a chauffeur
pull on his white gloves

Michael Thorley

~ ~ ~ ~

power surge –
driver's aged hands
svelte in red leather

Heather Gordon

~ ~ ~ ~

hiding
arthritic hands
lacy gloves

Ramah Juta

~ ~ ~ ~

on a stand
in the hardware shop
garden gloves
waiting in rows
to touch the soil

Michelle Brock

~ ~ ~ ~

a seed in my sock
the haiku moment
finds me

Greg Piko

~ ~ ~ ~

how come
it's happened again
this scourge
of the odd sock
haunting my laundry

Keitha Keyes

~ ~ ~ ~

old bedsock
gone from the washing line –
a new nest

Beatrice Yell

~ ~ ~ ~

monsoon deluge –
my slipper wedges
in the boardwalk

Samantha Sirimanne Hyde

~~~~

that's right
wear the old slippers
with holes in their toes –
a new pair in a box
waits to step into the world

Jo Tregellis

~~~~

adding poise
to her step
stilettos

Ramah Juta

~~~~

three pairs of shoes
three different sizes
duct tape mended
they walked from Syria
through borders to Germany

Sandra Renew

~ ~ ~ ~

hay shed clean-up
your old work boots
laced by spiders

Marietta McGregor

~ ~ ~ ~

no new cap
running shoes or T-shirt
just old boots
and the sound of silence
between each footstep

Kathy Kituai

~ ~ ~ ~

you gave me
rhinestones to wear
at the ball
so many Christmas beetles
outside the hall that night

Hazel Hall

soft grubs
amidst crisp mulberry leaves,
for your labours
I shall wear you to death
cocooned in memories

Sue MacKenzie

flamboyant red
a gladiolus reaching
for the stars –
it's not what she wears
but the way she wears it

Carole Harrison

~ ~ ~ ~

tightly tied
flannelette pyjamas
not the image
I had in mind after
your long absence

M.L. Grace

~ ~ ~ ~

blending
into her shiny hair
smoke curls
and Chanel no. 5
the scents of a mother

Frances Carleton

~ ~ ~ ~

goodbye hug
her scent on my jacket
all the way home

Lyn Reeves

~ ~ ~ ~

the past
is another country,
yet I wear
Worth's Je Reviens
hopefully…

Amelia Fielden

~ ~ ~ ~

budgie smugglers —
their life at the top
so brief

Bett Angel-Stawarz

~ ~ ~ ~

from under
my brief white tennis frock
I flashed
legs clad in scarlet tights…
just to see what might happen

Amelia Fielden

~ ~ ~ ~

active wear —
she reaches for a second
buttered bun

Lynette Arden

~ ~ ~ ~

ballet shoes
for him…soccer boots
for her
oh, how those twins
revel in diversity

Cynthia Rowe

~ ~ ~ ~

martial arts suit
with a simple yellow belt
my stepdaughter's
triumphant stance
another step closer to black

Bett Angel-Stawarz

~ ~ ~ ~

umbrellas
break from station doors
cloudburst

Kate King

~ ~ ~

city storm
my flimsy umbrella
liposuctions to a leaf

Scott Thouard

~ ~ ~

suitcase
not on the carousel
arrived home
with only my handbag
still…more than a refugee

Catherine Smith

~ ~ ~

nine months
the elastic gone
in my maternity pants

Vanessa Proctor

~ ~ ~ ~

on the way
to the operating theatre
dressed only
in a hospital gown
no room for false modesty

Keitha Keyes

~ ~ ~ ~

clad in sterile white
bedside shadows linger…
I daydream
adorn cloth of spun gold
this fine thread my link

Irene Bakker

~ ~ ~ ~

black hat…black coat
knee breeches protect him
from the heat
of the Holy City
and the twenty-first century

Gerry Jacobson

~ ~ ~ ~

through candle-glow
and incense fragrance
drifting down the aisle
a choir of boy sopranos
in angelic white robes

Rhonda Byrne

~ ~ ~ ~

saffron robes
shiny shaven head –
a boy sits
reciting prayers
not yet by heart

Barbara Curnow

~ ~ ~ ~

old house
clad in mottled brick
showing the wear
of many hurried feet
on its stone steps

Maria Encarnacao

~ ~ ~ ~

she wears
only what is comfortable
on the patio
a light breeze in her hair,
sunshine on her skin

Kathy Kituai

~ ~ ~ ~

I remember
the smile you wore
 when we met
all those years ago
on the nudist beach

Ken Sheerin

Contributing Poets

Angel-Stawarz, Bett
Arden, Lynette
Bakker, Irene
Benjamin, Anne
Brock, Michelle
Broughton, Belinda
Bruce, Dawn
Byrne, Rhonda
Carleton, Frances
Cottier, Penelope
Curnow, Barbara
Dean, Jan
Dorman, Christopher
Encarnacao, Maria
Ferguson, Glenys
Fielden, Amelia
Foster, Jan
George, Beverley
Gilbey, David
Gordon, Heather
Gower, Jill
Grace, M.L.
Graham, Janne
Hall, Hazel
Hanson, Simon
Harpeng, Jeffrey
Harrison. Carole
Hennessy, Gail
Holcombe, James
Holland, Lois
Humbert, Marilyn
Hyde, Samantha Sirimanne
Ingram, Teresa
Jacobson, Gerry
Juta, Ramah
Keyes, Keitha
King, Kate
Kituai, Kathy
Le Rossignol, Jane
MacKenzie, Sue
Mahony, Margaret
McGrath, Catherine
McGregor, Marietta
Miller, Mark
Ogi, Saeko
Pieloor, Janette
Piko, Greg
Proctor, Vanessa
Reeves, Lyn
Renew, Sandra
Rowe, Cynthia
Ruckert, Margaret Owen
Sheerin, Ken
Smith, Catherine

Smith, Crys
Summers, Carmel
Summerson, Rupert
Taylor, Barbara A.
Thorley, Michael
Thouard, Scott

Tregellis, Jo
Watcyn-Jones. Joanne
Williams, Rodney
Williamson, Paul
Yell, Beatrice
Zaknic, Athena

Acknowledgements

Some of the poems in this anthology have appeared previously in the following publications::
Bright Stars: an organic tanka anthology, ed. M. Kei, USA, 2014, 'this baby', Belinda Broughton
Eucalypt: a tanka journal, ed. Beverley George, Australia, 2006–
   issue 8, 'no new cap', Kathy Kituai
   issue 12, 'in plastic bags' (slightly changed), Michael Thorley
          'large footprints', Saeko Ogi
          'she slips', Barbara Curnow
   issue 13, 'saffron robes', Barbara Curnow
   issue 14, 'across the dusk', Paul Williamson
          'ballet shoes', Cynthia Rowe
   issue 18, 'she wears', Kathy Kituai
Facebook, 'an arrest', Anne Benjamin
FreeXpression, ed. Peter Pike, Australia, 2015, 'on the hills hoist', Margaret Mahony
Magna Poets journal, ed. Aurora Antonovic, Canada, 2011, 'think of me', Amelia Fielden
Mint Tea From a Copper Pot & Other Tanka Tales, Amelia Fielden, Australia 2013, 'from under' and 'the past', Amelia Fielden
paper wasp journal, ed. Katherine Samuelowicz, Australia, 2014, 'nine months', Vanessa Proctor
Presence, ed. Martin Lucas, UK, 2012
   # 28, 'twilight', Vanessa Proctor
   # 45, 'no wonder', Barbara A. Taylor
Ribbons, journal of the Tanka Society of America, ed. David

Rice, USA, 2016, 'suitcase', Catherine Smith
Spinifex haiku, Beverley George, Australia, 2006, 'retirement'. Beverley George
Yellow Moon, ed. Beverley George, Australia 2000–2006,
   #14, 'goodbye hug', Lyn Reeves
   #15, 'removing the rings', Lyn Reeves
   #20, 'home', Michael Thorley
Stylus poetry journal, ed. Rosanna Licari, Australia, 2006, 'autumn carnival', Beverley George

www.ingramcontent.com/pod-product-compliance
Lightning Source LLC
Chambersburg PA
CBHW070935080526
44589CB00013B/1518